About the Author....

Douglas Macauley lives in San Francisco, California. He is a dedicated father with children spanning two generations: a daughter, age ten, and a son, age thirty. With degrees in electrical engineering and computer science, Douglas builds on a foundation of over three decades as an electrical engineer for his work as a mindfulness practitioner, life coach, and intuitive energy healer. Douglas believes mindfulness allows us to find our centers, inner peace, and harmony while being guided by our hearts and staying grounded in our truth, which ultimately leads us to live a joyful life.

I Am a Feeling Body

Body Awareness and Mindfulness for Children

By Douglas Macauley

Illustrated by Ariane Elsammak

About the Book.....

I Am a Feeling Body is an uplifting, empowering book exploring body awareness and mindfulness for children. Grounded in simplicity and guided by playfulness, this book centers on a boy and his two loving cats as they explore four essential steps toward instilling peace, harmony, happiness, and well–being into their daily lives. Their unique experiences and curiosity shape a greater mind and body awareness that leads to a profound sense of freedom and feeling of joy that grows inside them every day.

For my dear children, Mark and Madelyn, who will always live in my heart as they continually inspire me to be the most loving father I can be.

In memory of my sweet and loving cats, Licorice and Taffi, who always embodied unconditional love.

Note to Parents....

Empowering children through body awareness and mindfulness requires a solid foundation. There are four essential steps toward instilling peace, harmony, happiness, and well–being into our lives: grounding, centering, breathing, and feeling. As outlined in this book, these four steps are designed to be enjoyed in a playful manner—and in less than ten minutes.

The word *instill* means to infuse slowly or gradually into the *mind* or *feelings*. We will go *inward* and find our *stillness* through playfulness. When we create the space each morning to engage ourselves in these steps, especially if family members participate in the fun together, we create profound results—a stronger mind and body connection to start us on our way each day.

Although this book is intended primarily for children, it is no less valuable for any age group. Have your child read this book out loud for the first time to an adult or caretaker. After that, it is most beneficial for someone to read the book to the child to enrich the experience of performing the exercises.

When the initial meanings in each of the four poems are absorbed cognitively and somatically as one, the benefits grow exponentially. Children will deepen their own awareness and become ready to read the book independently. The feelings children associate with seeing the illustrations will become somatic bookmarks for grounding, centering, breathing, and feeling.

When you lead your children through the exercises, allow them to discover the fun on their own terms and create unique personal experiences. Your children will find their way as their bodies guide them, and there is no right or wrong way. Trust and allow—amazing things will happen.

Grounding

Be Like a Tree

Sit in a special place that is relaxing to you.

Your body will feel good and know what to do.

Now think of a tree you'd like to be.

Close your eyes, and be that tree.

Your tree may be tall, flexible, or wide.

It's entirely your choice, so you can decide.

See your roots growing as the earth supports you.

Your body's foundation is strengthening too.

Feel both of your feet planted onto the floor.

Stretch your whole body as you ground even more.

The deeper your roots travel into the ground,
Your body will feel solid as the earth wraps around.

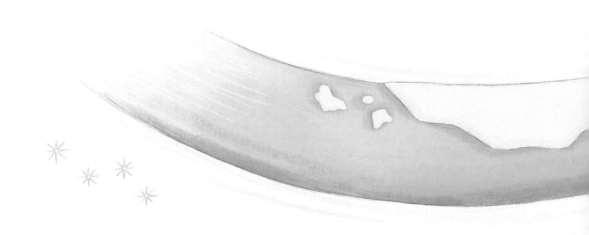

Your power resides within this place.

Claim it and own it for this is your space.

Centering

Find Your Dot

Sit or stand in your quiet place.

Relax your body, mind, and face.

Close your eyes and look inside.

Feel the amazing space to reside.

In your body, find the dot

That marks your body's center spot.

Perhaps your dot is near your heart.

This is the place you want to start.

Feel your body shrink in size.

Sit on your dot as you open your eyes.

You're in the center, calm as can be.

Feeling so strong, your worries are free.

Remind yourself of feeling this way

As you are centered every day.

Breathing

In and Out

Relax your body and close your eyes.

Feel the tension run down your thighs.

Fun in the Sun!

Take a deep breath, filling your lungs with air.

Slowly release it as you become more aware.

Slow down your breath as you breathe in once more.

Your body needs time for your breath to explore.

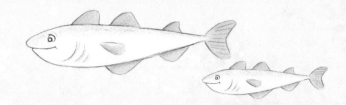

Stay focused with feeling as your breath takes a tour.

Know very deeply you are safe and secure.

Grounded and centered as your breath leads the way,

Your body is peaceful, yet it knows how to play.

Now all of your parts are working together.

Your whole body will feel light as a feather.

Feeling
Head to Toes

Find your special place for you to begin.

You continue your journey to feeling within.

Close your eyes, feel the stillness, but be very aware.

Your body has sensations so let us prepare.

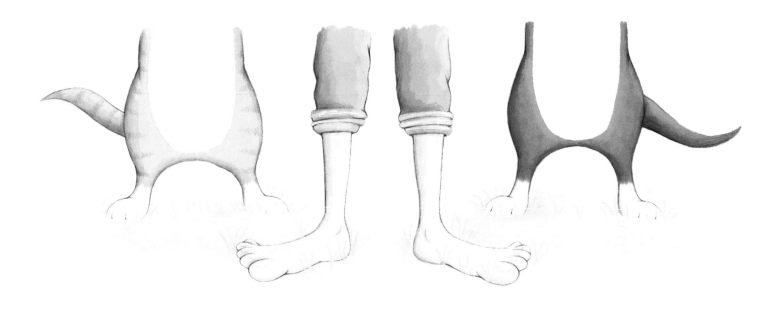

Start at your toes as your feet might agree.

Look, feel, and listen, but sit patiently.

Allow all of your senses to scan you inside.

Which one of your body parts is unwilling to hide?

It might be your knee, hip, shoulder, or head.

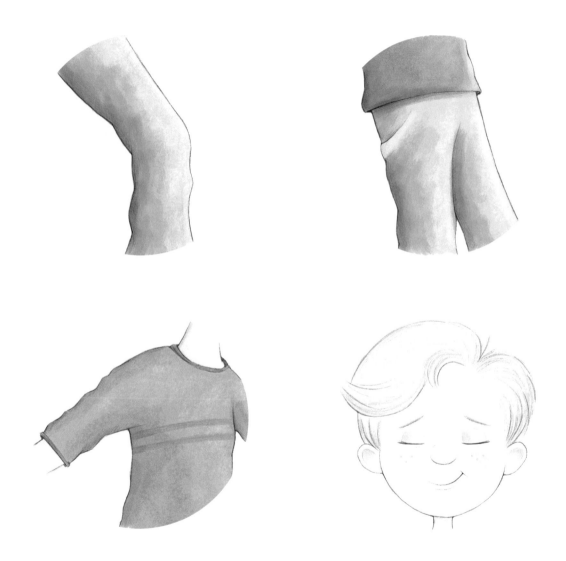

Let yourself feel it so your awareness will spread.

This sensation you feel is a sign you are living.
Be friends with it because your body's so giving.

Feeling your body and connecting inside
Is the most precious gift as you go for a ride.

Hooray! You have discovered more feelings in you.
You now have the tools to know what to do.

Putting It All Together

The deeper you ground, the more solid you feel.

This powerful feeling becomes very real.

When you center and ground and feel very strong,
Your body will be happy and not steer you wrong.

Adding your breath like a soft flowing breeze

Will let you live life with calmness and ease.

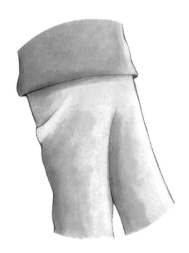

The more you feel the sensations within,
Your energy flows so your body will win.

Enjoy every moment in every day.

Know you are joy in every possible way.

Balboa Press books may be ordered through booksellers or by contacting:

Balboa Press
A Division of Hay House
1663 Liberty Drive
Bloomington, IN 47403
www.balboapress.com
1 (877) 407-4847

Because of the dynamic nature of the Internet, any web addresses or links contained in this book may have changed since publication and may no longer be valid. The views expressed in this work are solely those of the author and do not necessarily reflect the views of the publisher, and the publisher hereby disclaims any responsibility for them.

Any people depicted in stock imagery provided by Getty Images are models, and such images are being used for illustrative purposes only.
Certain stock imagery © Getty Images.

Interior Image Credit: Ariane Elsammak

ISBN: 978-1-9822-3405-8 (sc)
ISBN: 978-1-9822-3404-1 (e)

Library of Congress Control Number: 2019913049

Print information available on the last page.

Balboa Press rev. date: 09/04/2019

BALBOA.
PRESS
A DIVISION OF HAY HOUSE

Printed in the United States
By Bookmasters